My Book of Poems

Reflections of a young maiden's life on PEI during WWII

Jennie E. Smith,
Victoria West, PEI

Copyright © 2014 Robin (Nowell) Hartery.

Smith Nowell Hartery Publishing

All rights reserved. No part of this book may be reproduced, stored, or transmitted by any means—whether auditory, graphic, mechanical, or electronic—without written permission of both publisher and author, except in the case of brief excerpts used in critical articles and reviews. Unauthorized reproduction of any part of this work is illegal and is punishable by law.

ISBN: 978-0-578-14924-0 (sc)
ISBN: 978-1-4834-1964-0 (e)

Because of the dynamic nature of the Internet, any web addresses or links contained in this book may have changed since publication and may no longer be valid. The views expressed in this work are solely those of the author and do not necessarily reflect the views of the publisher, and the publisher hereby disclaims any responsibility for them.

Any people depicted in stock imagery provided by Thinkstock are models, and such images are being used for illustrative purposes only.
Certain stock imagery © Thinkstock.

Lulu Publishing Services rev. date: 10/20/2014

DEDICATION

This poetry was composed by my mom, Jennie,
and published in her memory.

PREFACE

This collection of poems was composed by my mother Jennie, who is no longer with us.

I am publishing Jennie's poetry to honor her and share her verse with others. Her poems are heartfelt reflections of a young maiden who, in her own words, was "a very serious and religious thinker and a very serious person."

Jennie was inspired by the beauty of Prince Edward Island, her home near the shore, and her loving family. She was also deeply affected by World War II and the sacrifices of the RCAF. During the 1940s, Jennie wrote poetry about God, nature, and the war. Many of her poems were composed by the side of Ellerslie brook in 1944.

Jennie was born and raised in Victoria West, PEI, where she lived with her parents William and Joanna (Ladner) Smith, her brother Roy, and sisters Stella, Mildred, and Gladys. Jennie taught school in Victoria West, Ellerslie, and Springhill in the 1940s after attending Bedeque College and Prince of Wales College. She was proud to be a "true blue" Prince Edward Islander.

Jennie moved to the US in 1946 to stay with her sister Stella. While visiting relatives in Somerville, MA, Jennie met Ralph E Nowell Jr, whom she married in 1949. They settled in historic Lexington, MA, where they raised their three children Randy, Robin, and Rhonda.

Jennie E. Smith
1923 – 2014

ACKNOWLEDGEMENT

I would like to thank my husband, Tom, for his support and my dear friend and colleague, Beth Kosis, who assisted with editing.

CONTENTS

CHAPTER 1
God and Family

To Our Island Home 2
Home 3
A Walk with God 4
Winter Thanks 5
Yuletide Thoughts 6
My Reverie 7

CHAPTER 2
Wonders of Nature

Down on the Countryside 10
June 11
An Autumn Day 12

CHAPTER 3
Sacrifices of the RCAF

A Soldier's Farewell 14
To Canadian Airmen 15
A Maiden's Letter to Her Soldier Sweetheart 16
In Memoriam 17
A Soldier's Thoughts 18
Onward Canadians 19
Ode to a Gallant Soldier 20
A Sacred Memory 21
Thoughts in the Night 22
Hope and Trust 23

CHAPTER 1

God and Family

To Our Island Home

In this fair province of our own,
We're proud to call Our Island Home.
With shady lanes and sunny nooks,
And all you read about in books.

Its pretty views, its splendour grand,
And Godly people seeking good,
A daughter of our motherland,
For whom are shed, our tears and blood.

We lend to thee our hearts our hands,
And all that wealth that we might own,
That we might live in peace, as just,
And keep secure Our Island Home.

Home

Home is a place that is perfect,
One's sorrows and joys are a share,
Of each understanding companion,
Who dwells in that circle there.

Our mother so kind and so gentle,
Watches o'er us with loving care,
And father, the head of the family,
Presides o'er that circle there.

Our sisters and brothers surround us,
With laughter and music that cheer,
And everyone feels so happy,
In that family circle so dear.

And God dominates in that family,
That's so happy and Godly and good,
And that, Love, Faith, and Hope is needed,
To have a home, as all Christians should.

A Walk with God

While walking down the old familiar way,
I caught a glimpse of God at close of day.
I saw him in the leaves all gold and brown,
I saw him on the scattered thistle down.

I saw him where the horses' feet had trod,
I saw him on the dampened upturned sod,
I saw him in the brook that wends close by,
I saw him where the earth would meet the sky.

I saw him in the moonlight o'er the rill,
I saw him on each hollow and each hill,
As step by step my homeward way I trod,
I felt that I was walking with my God.

[October 12, 1945. Composed while coming down from Aunt Flossie's house.]

Winter Thanks

For cheery fires and blanket warm,
For cozy shelter in the storm;
For those who all the winder through
Work willingly for me and you.

Who bring the groceries and the meat
To all the houses on our street;
For those who bring the coal we need,
The evening paper that we read.

For milkmen always neat and clean,
Who bring us daily milk and cream;
For those who clean away the snow
So we to work and school may go.

Dear God, we thank thee for these things;
For all the blessings each day brings.

Yuletide Thoughts

As the snow is softly falling
Down upon the native land,
And the blessed Christmastide is drawing near,
I think of you, my loved ones,
In our home upon the hill,
And I long to be there with you family dear.

Now on this Christmas Day,
I wish you every joy,
And I pray that the dear children's joys o'er brim,
As I think of our dear Saviour,
Who on Christmas Day was born,
In the lowly stable of a humble inn.

Dear Mother, though I've wandered,
Far from your tender care,
And I won't be with you on this Christmas Day;
My thoughts are ever with you,
You grow dearer day by day,
And I pray that God will bless you down life's way.

Dear Dad, I miss you also,
You're the dearest of all dads,
Your example helps me choose the narrow way;
I pray that you are happy,
And God will keep you safe,
Till I'm in my own dear home again to stay.

My Reverie

Alone I sit in solitude,
Down by the reeds on the shore,
And ponder o'er childhood and yesteryears,
That I shall know no more.
As I sit here in silent reverie,
Where the river wends its way,
I admire the picture nature paints,
On this beautiful Sabbath day.

Above me be-decked in azure blue,
The clouds swiftly sail on their way.
The sea is wearing its blue-green gown,
And white boats sail o'er the bay.
The trees are dressed in forest green,
And seagulls are soaring around,
As the sun slowly sinks to its home in the west,
All crimson and gold o'er the sound.

And I see my quaint little home o'er the hill,
Midst grain fields golden brown,
And the "old shore road" that leads me home,
Which has long since been trodden down.
As I wake from my golden reverie,
Where I sit on the sun kissed sod,
Me thinks how beautiful to behold,
Are the wonderful works of God.

CHAPTER 2

Wonders of Nature

Down on the Countryside

I hear the clang of the old cow bell,
The baa of the grazing sheep.
The friendly bark of a nearby dog,
And a little chicken's "peep."
The neighing sound of a tired horse,
A song two lovers are singing.
As the beautiful sun is sinking low,
I admire nature's designing.

The field's richly clad in their green attire,
The trees with their spreading limbs.
The hills they scan o'er the countryside,
And the brook with its joy o'er brims.
The shady lane where the sun peeps through,
The cottage down by the shore.
Just to sit and look at this beautiful scene,
Now who could desire more?

Now the moon steals o'er the countryside,
With it's magic of heavenly beauty.
And it lights the pleasant way to "Home Sweet Home,"
Where he rests from his daily duty.
It sends its beams o'er the cooing lovers,
And acts as a cupid's arrow.
And I think of the one who designed it all,
He, who loveth even a sparrow.

June

All the world is gay in June,
Flowers, birds, and all in tune,
Every day so full of joy,
For each little girl and boy.

Around the park they romp and play,
Swinging, swimming, all the day,
Till dost come the even tide,
With the sandman's lullaby.

When to their homes they quietly go,
Eager now for rest, but oh!
When the morning comes again,
What fun to play in sunny June.

An Autumn Day

Nature has painted a picture,
Of this beautiful ancient earth,
The birds that dwell in the tree tops,
O'erflow with their song of mirth.

The leaves are changing their costume,
From a beautiful green to gold,
The grain in the fields is ripened,
And the sheep wander out of the fold.

The brook still flows on its journey,
O'er bushes and crags and rills,
The ploughman shirks not his duty,
But upturns the vales and hills.

The clouds in their heavenly azure,
Roll on in their carefree way,
The sun completes the picture,
On this beautiful autumn day.

In these days of war and turmoil,
We should thank the good God above,
Who gives us such peace and beauty,
And unceasing wonderful love.

[September 22, 1943. Composed by the side of Ellerslie brook at noon hour while teaching there.]

CHAPTER 3

Sacrifices of the RCAF

A Soldier's Farewell

Although 'tis soon dear we must part,
Let's wear a smile and do our part,
The way seems dark and cloudy too,
But with God's help we shall pull through,
Until this war is over.

Although I may be long away,
I'll think of you dear every day,
And going down life's wary way,
I'll pray for God to speed the day,
This turmoil will be over.

I'll miss your smile dear when I go,
To fight for Right, 'gainst Freedom's foe,
As duty calls dear I must go,
But I'll come back again you know,
When the war is over.

To Canadian Airmen

You soaring rovers of the sky,
I envy you your office high,
You glide up through the air so free,
And nearer God you seem to be.

In working for our godly king,
You must be proud that you can say,
You work not only for King George,
But King of King and Lord of Lords.

You speak to me of something true,
Something mighty you could do,
So to you each and all I say,
Serve your King and God always.

A Maiden's Letter to Her Soldier Sweetheart

Tonight I am lonesome for you dear,
The one that I cherish and love.
You only can give me the happiness,
Bestowed by the good God above.

You are all the world to me dearest,
My thoughts are always of you.
You live in my every dream dear,
And may God make that dream to come true.

Without you dear, life would be empty,
And only a burden to bear.
So, please God give us each other,
Are the words of my every prayer.

In Memoriam

Dear brother since you're taken from our midst,
We've missed you more than words could e'er express.
And memories of one year ago today,
Brings longing for you in our hearts a-fresh.

'Twas then dear brother that we got the word,
That God had called you to his Golden Shore.
Although on earth we can ne'er meet again,
In heaven we shall meet to part no more.

[In loving memory of my dear brother in-law Harrison Craig, who passed away in Newfoundland on December 2, 1942 while serving king and country.]

A Soldier's Thoughts

Here on the battlefield darling,
Thinking only of you,
The shadows of evening are falling,
And the sun sets in crimson and blue.

I recall your beautiful countenance,
The tenderness of your love,
And to hold you once more in my arms dear,
Is my prayer to the good God above.

Although you are far from me darling,
And I'm here in this war-torn land,
Your spirit is ever so near me,
And I long for the touch of your hand.

But if God should call me away dear,
Before I return to my land,
I shall die with your name on my lips dear,
And we'll meet on that Golden Strand.

Onward Canadians

What keeps we Canadians fighting,
Through sweat, blood, and toil, and tears?
It's the flag of our British Empire
Which proudly has waved for years.

What keeps us plunging onward,
When everything spells defeat?
It's faith in our Heavenly Father,
Who reigns from his "mercy seat."

Why do our loved ones perish,
And die on a foreign land?
It's for "The Emblem of Canada,"
The banner, that ever will stand.

So, fight on brave Canadians! Fight boys!
Your fighting is not in vain,
You die upholding the right boys,
The world's freedom shall be your gain.

Ode to a Gallant Soldier

Down by the brook dear,
Where we used to roam,
I'm sitting here thinking of you, o'er the foam.
Of how you so gallantly, answered your call,
To fight for the freedom, we can never let fall.

Although you have gone dear,
And we're oceans apart,
Remember my darling,
That you're deep in my heart.
And though years may roll by dear,
Before our dreams can come true,
I'll never forget dear,
These sweet memories of you.

If perchance God should call you,
To his Heaven so rare,
Before you return dear,
From the fight over there.
I'll have known you and loved you,
And thank God above,
To have had such a blessing
As your wonderful love.

[May 23, 1944. Composed by the side of Ellerslie brook at noon hour shortly after Bill Conry of North Hamilton, Ontario volunteered for overseas duty in the Marine division of the RCAF.]

A Sacred Memory

We are sorry to inform you,
Was the message that she read,
That your true love who was wounded,
Is now reported dead.
He was wounded in the battle,
And before death closed his eyes,
His last words were tell my darling,
That I will meet her in the skies.

As she laid away the message,
Her eyes were filled with tears,
For the one she loved so truly,
For so many, many, years.
Had died to save his country,
That our flag fore'er might wave,
O'er the dear land of our freedom,
And the birthplace of our brave.

So! She bent her head in sadness,
And she knelt down there in tears,
Asking God to give her courage,
To continue through the years.
And though many battles may be won,
And peace come to her land,
She will ne'er forget her hero,
Lying on that foreign strand.

[May 24, 1944. Composed by the side of Ellerslie brook noon hour.]

Thoughts in the Night

In the stillness of night as I'm sitting,
Here by the side of my bed,
I watch from my window the heavens,
That so brightly shines overhead.

The moon rolls on, in its glory,
The stars seem to look and nod,
And the magic of all this kingdom,
Speaks of the glory of God.

And I think of all things beautiful,
Of how God created all,
With his grace and wonderful blessing,
He gave man domain o'er it all.

But my thoughts are soon interrupted,
By the clangour of shooting guns,
Made by the boys of our forces,
Who are training to fight the Huns.

Then the beautiful thought passes from me,
And I think, oh God, how soon,
These boys in bloody battle,
Will be under the same pale moon,

Not in such peaceful surroundings,
But amid war and toil and pain,
And I pray, oh God, please grant us
The blessing of peace once again.

Hope and Trust

Through this turmoil, blood, and sweat,
Help us dear Lord to not forget.
That Thou art over all always,
To guide the world in its dark days.

Nothing that Thine eye can't see,
Nothing that Thine ear can't hear,
Nothing that Thine hand can't do.
So help us Lord to worship Thee.

Help us to cast on Thee our cares,
And lay aside our foolish fears.
For Thou who wast our father's God,
Will be our God through all the years.

www.ingramcontent.com/pod-product-compliance
Lightning Source LLC
Chambersburg PA
CBHW031439040426
42444CB00006B/892